Published by the
Wilmington Star-News Inc.
Wilmington, N.C.

Edited by Bobby Parker

On the cover: Glen
Reinhart and Steve
Thomas crawl to safety
as waves pushed by
Hurricane Bertha
slam a dock at
Airlie Marina in
Wrightsville Beach
on July 12, 1996.

Photo by Todd Sumlin
Title design by Robert Holst

ISBN 0-9655164-0-7

The SAVAGE Season

Contents:

Hurricane Bertha slapped Southeastern North Carolina on July 12, 1996. Her big sister, Hurricane Fran, punished the area just eight weeks later on September 5.

If you have never been in one, it's just not possible to imagine the raging, destructive power of a hurricane.

Many residents of Wilmington and the beaches had moved into the area in the past few years and had never experienced a hurricane. Many natives had never faced the fury of a storm as strong as Fran.

The damage from the hurricane winds and accompanying flooding totaled in the hundreds of millions of dollars. Lives were lost. The emotional stress from two hurricanes so close together lingered long after the winds died.

This book is a story of Bertha and Fran in words and pictures by the writers and photographers of the Morning Star and Sunday Star-News.

John A. Lynch
Publisher,
Wilmington Morning Star

Hurricane Bertha ate chunks of Secondary Road 1568 at North Topsail Beach. The road was moved back from the oceanfront several years ago partly to avoid overwash and partly so developers could build beachfront condos.

TYLER HICKS

JAMIE MONCRIEF

Jim Tubman and
5-year-old
Kayla Ihlefield
settle in Sept. 6
at an evacuation
shelter at South
Brunswick High
School. They fled
Long Beach as
Hurricane Fran
approached.

TYLER HICKS

STORM SURGE

In Bertha's wake, Hurricane Fran sets new standard for destruction

By SCOTT WHISNANT

Fran visited Sept. 5 and did some rear-ranging.

Beach cottages were smashed into rubble, and roads were eaten away. Refrigerators and cars became floating debris.

Whole towns were submerged, piers broke away, and beach dunes were flattened and dumped into streets.

Boats were crushed and crops were leveled. Trees snapped in two. A church's steeple tumbled to the ground.

For days, thousands of Southeastern North Carolina residents were forced to live without air conditioning, hot water and refrigeration.

The storm killed 38 people -- 25 in North Carolina -- and scared countless others.

"I sure had a lot of religion last night," said Brenda Baker of Wilmington. "Every time I heard a noise, I started praying."

But the hurricane's most remarkable feat may have been rewriting history.

For generations to come, the benchmark hurricane will no longer be only Hazel of 1954. Years from now, when people living in the region want to remind friends and relatives what a *real* storm was like, they'll talk about Hurricane Fran.

And the punch line will be this: Fran was not the first storm of 1996. For only the second time in state history, the eyes of two hurricanes spun along almost the same path in the same summer, rekindling the regional nickname "Hurricane Alley."

Hurricanes Connie and Ione hit Morehead City in 1955.

The lore of the summer of '96 will be more than memories and anecdotes of those who lived through a savage season. The coastline will never look the same. The storms destroyed so many beachfront houses in environmentally sensitive areas that a debate raged on how, or whether, they would be rebuilt.

TYLER HICKS

Kenny Batts was open for business Sept. 16 at his grill in Surf City, despite major damage by Hurricane Fran. That's the roof from the firehouse next door smashed atop his restaurant.

Bertha, a Category 2 storm that barreled in on July 12, was the first hurricane to directly hit the area since Diana in 1984. The storm did significant damage, about $38 million.

"If I live to see another one, I'm heading for the hills," said 78-year-old Doris Culverhouse, who rode out Bertha in her Carolina Beach home with her husband, Bill.

No one would guess then that three more hurricanes would threaten the Carolina coast in the next nine weeks. Edouard spun just east of the coast around Labor Day weekend. Fran hit a few days later. Hortense threatened the next week, but it also turned north just in time.

By then Fran, a Category 3 storm, had reduced Bertha to a footnote.

'IT WAS JUST LIKE A DOG SHAKING A RAG DOLL. WE WERE JUST WHIPPING AT THE END OF A CHAIN.'

Richard Matthews, pilot of the *Utopia*. The yacht got caught in the thick of Fran when its owner, thinking the storm would hit farther south, was moving it from Myrtle Beach to Wilmington

Preceding page: What's left of the Kure Beach Pier after Hurricane Bertha reduced it to a pile of planks.

A bulldozer pushes up sand Sept. 12 at the Fort Fisher-Kure Beach line, where the beach was battered by Hurricane Fran.

"We had a little breeze come by here on July 12th," said Dave Clark, Onslow County public works director. "This was a *real* storm."

Real indeed.

"It's breathtaking," said John Carty of Carolina Beach. "When you see a whole hotel washed in the ocean, that gives you a whole new perspective."

Beyond the estimated $6.57 billion in damage, the 60,000 destroyed or damaged homes, the ruined boats and those left homeless, Fran brought personal tragedy.

Three Marines driving toward the high-rise bridge leading to North Topsail Beach were swept off the road into a raging sound. They held on to each other, but two were washed away. One crawled back on land and found help; another died. The third Marine grabbed a tree, where he was found about nine hours later.

In Duplin County, a Rose Hill woman was crushed as her chimney fell through her roof and onto her couch. A man in Scotts Hill helping a friend board up his house was carried

away by the storm surge and drowned.

An elderly, bedridden woman in Surf City was found in a marsh floating on her mattress after her mobile home was smashed. She died days later.

For most, the storm hurt in smaller, but painful, ways. It took days for beach residents to get back to their homes and weeks for the beaches to reopen to the public.

Wrightsville Beach, which had taken comfort in how little damage Bertha caused, was the last New Hanover County beach town to reopen.

The evacuees returned to sobering sights.

Topsail Island, including Topsail Beach, Surf City and North Topsail Beach, got the worst of it. Hardly any oceanfront houses escaped serious damage, especially the older cottages.

State officials estimated that as much as 90 percent of some beach areas was destroyed.

Some oceanfront homes simply dis-

LIFE ROPE

As the water rose around his North Topsail Beach home on the night of Sept. 5, Len Gioglio did the only thing he could think of: He tied a rope around himself, lashed it to his battered home, and held his dog in his arms for two terrifying hours as they were slammed by Hurricane Fran.

Each time the 4-foot storm surge slammed them down, Mr. Gioglio, 37, pulled himself and his dog back up, thinking the next time they might not make it.

"I thought I was going to die," Mr. Gioglio recalled.

Earlier in the day, his wife and two children sought shelter at Dixon Elementary School. Mr. Gioglio planned to complete storm preparations and join them. But he knew he had waited too late when he watched New Inlet Road, the only access to the northern-most tip of the island, begin to wash out.

As Fran came ashore, the house shook with the force of 105-mph winds, hurtling shingles and wood airborne.

"It was the worst night of my life."

JAMIE MONCRIEF

The storm washed away sea oats and other vegetation, the line from which construction setbacks are measured.

THE' N. PHAM

Dennis Newkirt tries to steer a car that was being pulled by an 18-wheeler on N.C. 53 near Maple Hill. Flooding made roads into rivers in the days after Hurricane Fran.

'I'VE GOT A PICKUP TRUCK SITTING ON MY FRONT PORCH.'

Bill Poe,
assistant fire marshal
at North Topsail Beach,
on the day after
Fran swept
through

Bicyclists detour around a house that was blown off its foundation by Hurricane Fran, landing about 200 feet away in the middle of Canal Drive in Carolina Beach.

appeared. Others floated into roadways or just toppled or crumbled.

"Oh, honey, I never thought it would be like this," said a teary Jean Nunamacher at her Surf City condominium.

She found a wall buckled under a water-logged ceiling, insulation wrapped around a banister, sand covering her VCR, and her bed unmade.

Farther south, Kure Beach seemed to suffer the most. A section of Atlantic Avenue was gone, and most oceanfront houses were badly damaged.

Carolina Beach was under 6 feet of water at times. One man, who thought waves were breaking up his condominium building, called 911 to relay a message to his next of kin. During the height of the storm, firefighters had to scramble to find higher ground.

"I don't know what we're going to do," said Kelly Goeller as she checked her condo on Florida Avenue. "There's debris everywhere. It looks like a bomb exploded."

Almost all of Wrightsville Beach was underwater at some point. Residents of Harbor Island found high-water lines 4 feet above the floor.

Three days after the storm, antsy property owners wanted to get back on the beach, mostly to secure their homes from rainstorms forecast for the next three days.

Mayor Herb McKim met an angry mob at the drawbridge and told them through a megaphone to be patient. The crowd hooted

'IT'S BREATHTAKING. WHEN YOU SEE A WHOLE HOTEL WASHED IN THE OCEAN, THAT GIVES YOU A WHOLE NEW PERSPECTIVE.'

John Carty, who had to shout to communicate with his family in their Carolina Beach home because Fran's winds were so loud

in derision.

The damage proved to be far more than roofs, furniture and appliances. Anything left at floor level was ruined, and that often included things money can't replace -- wedding and baby photos, favorite videos and children's drawings.

Part of the "trash" was piled at curbside, along with broken chairs and soaked carpet. While debris haulers went to work, bulldozers piled sand covering the streets back into dunes

Up and down the coast, marina docks either floated off or were twisted. And the damage was just beginning for businesses.

Hoping for a big September to make up for Bertha, hotels and restaurants instead realized the tourist season had pretty much come to an end.

Somehow Brunswick County, where Fran first made landfall, was spared serious damage caused by winds to the north and northeast of the eye. Weeks later, the county's beach hotels were jammed with tourists who had canceled vacations farther north.

Inland, crop damage was even worse than Bertha's, although much had been harvested. But tobacco that was being cured was ruined because of the loss of power.

A few days after Fran, people living near the Northeast Cape Fear River in Pender and Duplin counties had another problem. Four inches of rain, added to the 6 inches that fell during the hurricane, caused the river to jump its banks and flood to its highest levels in memory.

Post-hurricane rains flooded the region. In Brunswick County, four days after Fran schoolchildren were sent home early so their families could find higher ground

In Columbus County, fiercely independent residents of Crusoe Island refused to leave, even after rising water cut them off from emergency services.

The Northeast Cape Fear crested Sept. 11 after as much as 18 feet of flooding in some places.

Fran's damage went beyond rising water and high wind. After two storms in one sum-

Buck Engle patches his sister-in-law's house in Burgaw. Fran crashed five trees onto the roof.

mer, residents simply got tired of the hurricane routine.

At first they pulled together. Neighbors visited as they cleaned their yards together and later had cookouts so they could eat food before it spoiled.

In Wilmington, a surprise wedding for a couple who had married earlier in Germany continued as planned the day after the storm. The party managed without electricity in 90-degree heat, as chain saws whined in the background.

Kurt Mittag, a native of Germany who thought he was coming to North Carolina for a vacation, said he and his German friends

water," said Sharon Helton, who had almost finished cleaning Bertha debris at her Middle Sound area home when Fran knocked more than 20 trees down. "You can't wash your hands, flush the toilet. You just feel dirty."

One sight consistently cheered everyone. Relief workers, including power workers and firefighters with chain saws, poured in from cities and states that remembered similar help during natural disasters in their hometowns.

Those from South Carolina remembered Hugo. The Floridians remembered Andrew.

Many beach homeowners are not in compliance with current zoning laws regarding how close they can build to the water's edge. Any owner who suffered damage exceeding half the value of the home must get a permit before rebuilding.

Also, beach towns lost the line of vegetation that marks the edge of waterfront lots. The new line may likely be moved back, farther from the water, which will reduce the size of lots. That means there's a real question if they will be allowed.

"We'll be ready for next tourist season," said Eric Peterson, town manager at Topsail Beach, where 62 homes were destroyed and hundreds were damaged. "But it'll be a different place. Topsail Beach won't ever look the same again."

At North Topsail Beach, the question practically came down to whether the town would survive.

Congress tried to discourage people from developing the area in 1982, saying the federal government would not reimburse for any damage there. But the town was developed anyway. When Bertha hit, federal regulators began wrestling with how much relief to offer and what could be rebuilt.

Before those questions were resolved, Fran came. Though the northern tip of the island wasn't damaged as much by Fran as by Bertha, much of the area Congress decided was non-buildable was wiped out.

The sticky situation will take months, maybe years, to resolve. Gov. Jim Hunt said he would wait until after the November 1996 election to tackle the issue.

KEN BLEVINS

Gina Simmons had planned to be married under this 200-year-old oak tree at her Hampstead home. Hurricane Fran ripped it from the ground.

were impressed.

"In this situation, only in America could you do this," he said. "In Germany we would sit in our cellars and worry."

But Reid Wilson, associate clinical professor at the University of North Carolina at Chapel Hill, predicted that more than two days of no power, ice or clean water would lead to stress, saying "we're not built to pay attention to that anymore."

Dr. Wilson's prediction was borne out. People waited hours to buy a $500 generator, a dollar bag of ice or a $5 breakfast and had fitful nights of sleep without air conditioning. Beach residents had trouble getting to their property and couldn't leave once they got there. Curfews cut short or ruled out a restaurant meal or movie.

"The worst thing is having kids with no

Those from California remembered earthquakes.

"I think Georgia Power has the greatest bunch of guys," said Charles Steel, a Country Club Road resident watching a crew work through a Sunday downpour. "It was pouring like the devil. I know they would rather be home watching a football game."

Unless you lived in one of the last areas to get power, the relief workers were everyone's heroes – so much so that when a dog show at Legion Stadium threatened to displace workers from their hotel rooms, there was an uproar.

But there were some problems that just couldn't be fixed. The legacy of Fran may not be its threat to Hazel as the state's worst natural disaster, but for its permanent effect on the coast.

Before it's over, Fran could make its way into several courtrooms.

On the beachfronts, Fran's legacy -- a condemned cottage waiting to be torn down, a mangled pier, a restaurant that never reopened – will be with us a long time. Things will get back to normal, but by then, most everyone in the region will have had enough of Fran, Bertha and the summer of '96.

Mable Earley, whose oceanfront cottage at North Topsail Beach was destroyed, summed it up for many:

"I think it's God's way of showing us who's boss."

Scott Whisnant is regional editor of the Wilmington Morning Star. This report includes material from other staff writers.

'I SURE HAD A LOT OF RELIGION IN ME LAST NIGHT. EVERY TIME I HEARD A NOISE, I STARTED PRAYING.'

Brenda Baker of Wilmington, who drove around town for an hour looking for ice the morning after Fran knocked out power

KEN BLEVINS

National Guardsmen patrol Atlantic Avenue in Kure Beach a week after Fran devastated the oceanside road.

Richard Gibbs reaches for his son, Keegan, who was caught in a gust of wind as Hurricane Bertha rolled into Southport at the mouth of the Cape Fear River.

Bertha's winds snatched a Navy ship from its mooring at Sigma Recycling on the Cape Fear River in Wilmington. It became stranded near Cape Fear Community College.

'I'M NOT BRAVE, I'M A CHRISTIAN. IT'S IN GOD'S HANDS NOW.'

Dixie Jones of Kure Beach, who sat in her car outside the shelter at Trask Middle School because she likes her privacy. Around 1:45 p.m., as the wind grew stronger, she had a change of heart and sought shelter inside

BERTHA BARRELS IN

Early-season hurricane packed a powerful punch

By SCOTT WHISNANT

Hurricane Bertha was the most talked-about storm in years as it spun up the Atlantic coast in mid-July.

Weather forecasters called it the largest July storm to threaten the Carolinas. As residents of Southeastern North Carolina watched satellite photos of the advancing storm, it started to look as though Bertha, after a series of misses from Gloria (1985), Hugo (1989) and Emily (1993), would be the first major storm to hit the area since Diana in 1984.

It couldn't have come at a worse time. During the week after the July 4th holiday, the height of tourist season, beach towns prepared to evacuate.

On Thursday, July 11, Bertha looked as though it would wobble west and hit Charleston, S.C. Area beach towns evacuated anyway, and the storm made two changes during the night: It weakened, and it turned north.

On Friday morning, July 12, it was clear that Bertha was headed to the Wilmington area. By midmorning, heavy winds were lashing the coast. The eye grazed Bald Head Island and passed over Kure Beach.

Bertha finally turned inland and made landfall between Wilmington and Sneads Ferry.

New Hanover, Pender and Onslow counties caught the northeast section of the storm, the strongest part, as Bertha barreled northward. Kure Beach officials reported that the wind had blown the roofs off three houses, many homes had some damage and the Kure Beach pier was gone.

The worst of Bertha hit an area that could least afford it – North Topsail Beach. The low-lying barrier island was developed in an area Congress had decided was unsafe to develop and would not help rebuild with federal money. Critics said a hurricane would ravage such a narrow island, and Bertha

TYLER HICKS

No one was inside this house on Fort Fisher Boulevard in Kure Beach when Hurricane Bertha ripped the roof off. Owner Kathy Woods begins the cleanup.

Topsail Island faced the strongest part of Hurricane Bertha -- the northeast section of the storm. The roof was ripped off this beachfront house, while neighboring homes had less severe damage.

RESCUE ME

At the height of Hurricane Bertha's strike on July 12, Surf City police rescued more than 50 people who changed their minds and decided not to brave the storm.

"We went to get a lady that was up at the north end, and we got out of the car trying to get to her house, and the roof picked up off her house and just missed the patrol car and us by about 6 feet," Police Chief David Jones said. "A whole roof crashed in the road in front of us."

No one was injured.

Town firefighters also found people begging to be rescued. As the wind tossed debris through the air and water rose across the road, a Fire Department patrol saw two people in the road waving a yellow sheet.

"It was crazy," said fire Capt. Robert Steffee. "I just can't believe we were actually here when this was happening."

would prove to be the first real test of that prediction.

The town didn't do too well.

Waves washed over the island's main road. Thousands of feet of pavement washed away, leaving craters big enough for cars to tumble into. Water lines were destroyed and sand dunes erased. More than 120 homes were destroyed.

The storm was bad throughout Onslow County. The gymnasium roof blew off at Dixon Middle School, which was an emergency shelter. Evacuees had to move to the cafeteria.

At 4 p.m., Jeff Hudson, Onslow County's acting emergency management director, hid behind his desk as he talked on the phone in Jacksonville.

"I'm telling you, this is rough," he said.

When it was over, farmers had sustained major crop damage and there was doubt whether the beach tourist economy could recover this year. Hotels looked to make up losses in the fall.

President Clinton designated 17 counties as disaster areas. The losses were an estimated $228 million, with about 1,100 homes

destroyed.

But the area bounced back quickly. By Monday, July 15, just about all the 113,000 people who had lost power had it restored. Other than the lingering effects in North Topsail Beach, where the debate was heating

'WE'RE GOING CRAZY IN HERE. PEOPLE ARE FLOCKING HERE FROM THE BEACHES, NEWS CREWS ARE COMING FROM TAMPA AND FREAKS ARE TRAVELING FROM OUT OF TOWN TO WATCH THE STORM.'

Wilbur Brown, manager of Wilmington's Best Western Carolinian motel

up over what the government would pay to rebuild, Bertha seemed destined for this unusual legacy: People swore they would never evacuate for a hurricane again.

The storm wasn't the Big One -- or even a bad one, for many. While a wind gust of 108 mph was recorded near North Topsail Beach, most of the area escaped hurricane-force wind. At the New Hanover County airport,

In Bertha's wake

Storm left a swath of downed trees, damaged houses

🌀 9 p.m. 7/12 **86 mph**

NEW HANOVER COUNTY

Areas outside city limits:
- $12.5 million in damage.
- $2 million in response cost.
- $1 million in mostly water damage at New Hanover Regional Medical Center.
- 1,480 houses damaged.
- 250 businesses damaged.

WILMINGTON

About $1 million total
- 108 houses damaged
- 26 businesses damaged
- Trees down.
- Power failures across the city.

BRUNSWICK BEACHES

Minimal damage

PLEASURE ISLAND

Kure Beach:
- Kure Beach Pier washed away.
- Widespread roof damage.

Carolina Beach:
- Carolina Beach Fishing Pier washed away.
- Recently replenished berm washed away.
- Parts of Carolina Avenue under 3 feet of sand.
- Many roofs damaged; many windows broken.
- Jubilee Park Ferris wheel demolished
- Sewage pumping station damaged; raw sewage flowed into street near Boardwalk.

ONSLOW COUNTY

- 127 houses destroyed countywide; figure does not include Jacksonville.
- $102.3 million in damage.

TOPSAIL BEACH

- 5 houses seriously damaged.
- 50 houses with minor damage.

NORTH TOPSAIL BEACH

- Several thousand feet of Secondary Road 1568 washed out at northern end.
- Ocean Bay Village condos seriously damaged.
- All power off on island.

WRIGHTSVILLE BEACH

- 75 feet lost from Johnnie Mercer's Fishing Pier.
- Some damage to pilings at Oceanic Pier.
- Widespread damage to roofs and piers.
- Damage to about 125 homes, $712,000 total.
- Erosion at Mason Inlet near Shell Island Resort.

BALD HEAD ISLAND/ SOUTHPORT

- Little damage reported.
- Whittler's Bench cedar destroyed in Southport.
- Superficial building damage to nuclear plant.

Jacksonville

New River

Onslow County

North Topsail Beach

Pender County

17 Surf City

Hampstead

Topsail Beach

New Hanover County

74 76

Wilmington

Wrightsville Beach

🌀 5 p.m. 7/12 **98 mph**

17 87

Brunswick County

211

Southport

Carolina Beach
Kure Beach

Long Beach

Holden Beach

Bald Head Island

Atlantic Ocean

Ocean Isle Beach

SOURCES: National Weather Service; National Hurricane Center; local governments

CAROL COLLIER

Hurricane Bertha tracking history

37.4, 76.5 / 5 a.m. 7/13
36.1, 77.2 / 1 a.m. 7/13
35.3, 77.5 / 9 p.m. 7/12
34.3, 77.7 / 5 p.m. 7/12
33.3, 78.0 / 1 p.m. 7/12
32.3, 78.5 / 8 a.m. 7/12
31.2, 78.6 / 2 a.m. 7/12
30.7, 78.2 / 8 p.m. 7/11
30.2, 78.1 / 2 p.m. 7/11
29.2, 77.4 / 8 a.m. 7/11
28.3, 76.9 / 2 a.m. 7/11
27.4, 76.3 / 8 p.m. 7/10
26.2, 76.1 / 2 p.m. 7/10
25.4, 75.4 / 8 a.m. 7/10
24.5, 73.9 / 2 a.m. 7/10
23.7, 72.6 / 8 p.m. 7/09
22.5, 71.0 / 2 p.m. 7/09
20.2, 67.9 / 3 a.m. 7/09
18.5, 64.8 / 2 p.m 7/08

Raleigh
N.C.
Wilmington
Myrtle Beach
Charleston
Savannah
Ga.
Jacksonville
Cape Canaveral
Fla.
Miami
Gulf of Mexico
Bermuda
Atlantic Ocean
Bahama Islands
Cuba
Caribbean Sea
Dominican Republic
Haiti
Puerto Rico

35°
30°
25°
20°

85°   80°   75°   70°   65°

CAROL COLLIER

A hurricane-tracking plane from the National Oceanic and Atmospheric Administration views the eye of Hurricane Bertha July 10 east of the Bahamas. The WP-3D Orion is based at MacDill Air Force Base in Tampa, Fla. It flew through the eye five times seeking clues about the storm's path.

ERNST PETERS / Lakeland (Fla.) Ledger

Carolina Beach residents began gathering at dawn July 13 at the Snows Cut bridge, anxious to see what damage their property had suffered during Hurricane Bertha. But many were dismayed and angered when town officials refused to let them back on the island until 6 p.m.

top sustained winds were 53 mph. The storm surge was 4 to 6 feet in most places, which flooded only parts of beaches.

So when beach officials kept their towns closed while cleanup began, residents were furious.

A man in North Topsail Beach wagged his finger in Mayor Marty Bostic's face and said, "This is the United States of America. I'll stay the next time."

In Carolina Beach, Town Manager George Rose declared, immediately after the hurricane, "They can line up all the way to Raleigh to get on this island. But it ain't happening."

The next day, residents appeared to be taking Mr. Rose up on his offer. Angry drivers at Snows Cut bridge couldn't get across. New Hanover County Commissioner Bill Caster and Sheriff Joe McQueen intervened on the residents' behalf.

The town, with a meager and outdated hurricane plan, seemed in disarray.

" 'Mad' is not the word. I'm flabbergasted," said resident Debbie Welch. "The purpose of any evacuation is to save life and limb. What this has done is create a mentality of people who will not leave the next time."

Eight weeks later, that mentality was forgotten.

THE LONG SWIM HOME

A day after Hurricane Bertha hit, tempers flared as government officials kept anxious residents from returning to the storm-battered beaches.

"Are we supposed to let people on the island with nails and raw sewage in the streets?" asked Carolina Beach Town Manager George Rose, who was barraged with arguments from homeowners demanding to get back on the island.

Some people posed as work crews and town employees in order to get across the Snows Cut bridge. Others abandoned their vehicles to walk across the bridge.

A few found more ingenious ways to return.

"It seemed like we were not getting any information from the officials," said Mark McHorney, 26, who with his brother decided to swim across the Intracoastal Waterway about 1:30 p.m. to check on their family's home.

Town officials reluctantly opened the island to residents about 6 p.m.

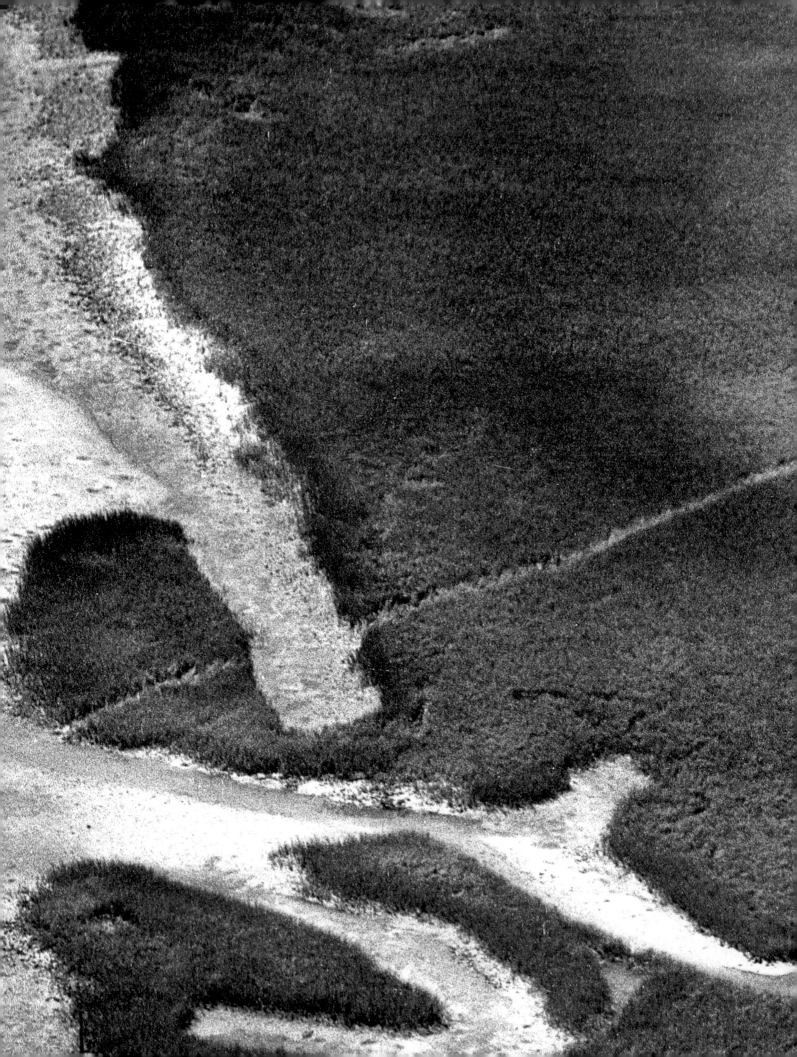

Raeford Brinkley's clock stopped after Bertha ripped the roof and a wall off his home on Fort Fisher Boulevard in Kure Beach.

Preceding page: A sailboat was blown into a marsh at Wrightsville Beach. TYLER HICKS

TYLER HICKS

He was not at home during the storm.

"I was devastated when I heard it," said Leila Pigott, who has lived in the same house in Southport for 53 years.

Residents and visitors to the picturesque town - some of them a bit teary-eyed - picked up pieces of the cedar tree at Whittler's Bench that had been downed by Hurricane Bertha.

A charter member of the Southport Garden Club, Mrs. Pigott had helped plant the cedar after Hurricane Hazel destroyed two poplar trees that grew there in 1954.

Men of the town used to sit on the bench under the cedar to whittle and gossip, she said.

KEN BLEVINS

Sand overwhelmed the Rex restaurant at St. Regis Resort in North Topsail Beach after Hurricane Bertha pushed through.

21

'IT EVEN SHUCKED THE CORN ON THE STALK.'

Emily Johnson, wife of Pender County farmer Joab Johnson, after Hurricane Fran

Jerry Willetts' cornfield on N.C. 87 in Brunswick County was flattened by Hurricane Bertha. Crop losses in the July storm were estimated at $140 million. Eight weeks later, Hurricane Fran dealt farmers a second devastating blow. Heavy losses were sustained on corn, cotton, tobacco and poultry farms.

TODD SUMLIN

Randy and Tina Parsons brave wind and rain as Hurricane Fran rages about 5 p.m. Sept. 5 on Lake Park Boulevard in Carolina Bea

FRAN SLAM

Destructive storm unleashed its fury on Carolina coast

By SCOTT WHISNANT

The weather talk of the Cape Fear region in early September was of a major hurricane. Its name was Edouard.

The large, Category 3 hurricane threatened to ruin the Labor Day weekend, just as Bertha had ruined the week after July 4. Forecasters noticed the storm didn't turn north as quickly as predicted, and beach towns again were warning residents and tourists that another evacuation may be on the way.

Two storms, Fran and Gustav, were trailing Edouard in the Atlantic. Fran reached hurricane strength, but forecasters said it would weaken in water cooled by Edouard. There was even a chance Fran would catch Edouard in the Atlantic, canceling both storms.

Edouard turned north in plenty of time, though many vacationers stayed away, marring Labor Day for area businessmen who wondered if the summer could get much worse. Fran was downgraded to a tropical storm.

But the next few days brought a terrible turn. A high pressure system in the north Atlantic pushed Fran toward the Georgia-South Carolina coast. And the storm was gaining strength.

By Thursday, Sept. 5, Fran was a well-organized Category 3 storm, but had drifted northward. It seemed likely to hit Myrtle Beach, S.C., and drew comparisons to Hugo, the huge storm of 1989 that devastated Charleston.

North Carolina beaches evacuated.

'WE HAD A LITTLE BREEZE COME BY HERE ON JULY 12TH. THIS WAS A REAL STORM.'

Dave Clark, Onslow County public works director, sizing up Hurricane Fran compared with Hurricane Bertha

As Thursday wore on, the prognosis changed from a brush with Fran-related winds to an unavoidable clash with the brunt of the storm. Fran, starting to look more like the legendary Hurricane Hazel of 1954, was headed here.

The storm moved toward land more quickly than anticipated. It made landfall around 8:45 p.m. near the mouth of the Cape Fear River in Southport, then basically followed the river's path. The eye passed over Wilmington around 9:30 p.m.

By increasing its speed, Fran timed its hit with a low tide. Had it kept its slower speed, it would have hit at high tide, and the storm surge would have been worse.

Area residents, now attuned to assessing hurricanes after Bertha's visit two months before, knew immediately Fran was different. Sustained winds of 90 mph or more hit the beaches, with gusts of more than 100 mph. A storm surge, as high as 11 feet at Mason Inlet north of Wrightsville Beach, flooded all of Topsail Island and practically all of Wrightsville Beach and Figure Eight Island.

Topsail Island got the worst of it. Damage estimates ranged as high as 90 percent of some areas -- though the north end of North Topsail Beach may have suffered more during Bertha. In Onslow County alone, 696 homes were destroyed, about a third of the overall statewide total of 1,953.

The storm even carried inland and wreaked major havoc on Raleigh, downing trees and power lines everywhere. When President Clinton flew in to survey the damage, he came to Raleigh, not the coast.

Overall, damage estimates on Fran continued to climb. The total was projected to reach $6.57 billion, one of the costliest storms of all time. More than 30,000 homes and almost 900 businesses were damaged, and the loss in timber was worth $1.2 billion alone. Agriculture losses were another $700 million.

President Clinton declared 51 counties disaster areas, and the argument reheated over whether federal money should rebuild North Topsail Beach, which Congress had deemed unsafe in 1982.

Most people waited several days and some several weeks for power. If not for the heroic efforts of out-of-town volunteers, the wait would have been much longer. People seemed more patient this time than they had in the Bertha aftermath, no doubt

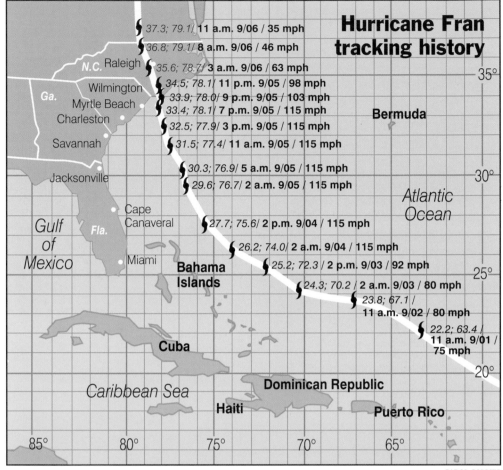

Hurricane Fran tracking history

37.3; 79.1/ 11 a.m. 9/06 / 35 mph
36.8; 79.1/ 8 a.m. 9/06 / 46 mph
35.6; 78.7/ 3 a.m. 9/06 / 63 mph
34.5; 78.1/ 11 p.m. 9/05 / 98 mph
33.9; 78.0/ 9 p.m. 9/05 / 103 mph
33.4; 78.1/ 7 p.m. 9/05 / 115 mph
32.5; 77.9/ 3 p.m. 9/05 / 115 mph
31.5; 77.4/ 11 a.m. 9/05 / 115 mph
30.3; 76.9/ 5 a.m. 9/05 / 115 mph
29.6; 76.7/ 2 a.m. 9/05 / 115 mph
27.7; 75.6/ 2 p.m. 9/04 / 115 mph
26.2; 74.0/ 2 a.m. 9/04 / 115 mph
25.2; 72.3/ 2 p.m. 9/03 / 92 mph
24.3; 70.2 / 2 a.m. 9/03 / 80 mph
23.8; 67.1 / 11 a.m. 9/02 / 80 mph
22.2; 63.4 / 11 a.m. 9/01 / 75 mph

CAROL COLLIER

TODD SUMLIN

'It's quite a nasty storm,' one forecaster said of Fran. Evacuees heeded that warning as they fled the coast bumper-to-bumper on College Road toward Interstate 40.

Preceding page: Oceanfront homes at North Topsail Beach were reduced to piles of rubble. KEN BLEVINS

Totaling THE damage

Local officials try to put a price tag on property losses in Hurricane Fran's aftermath

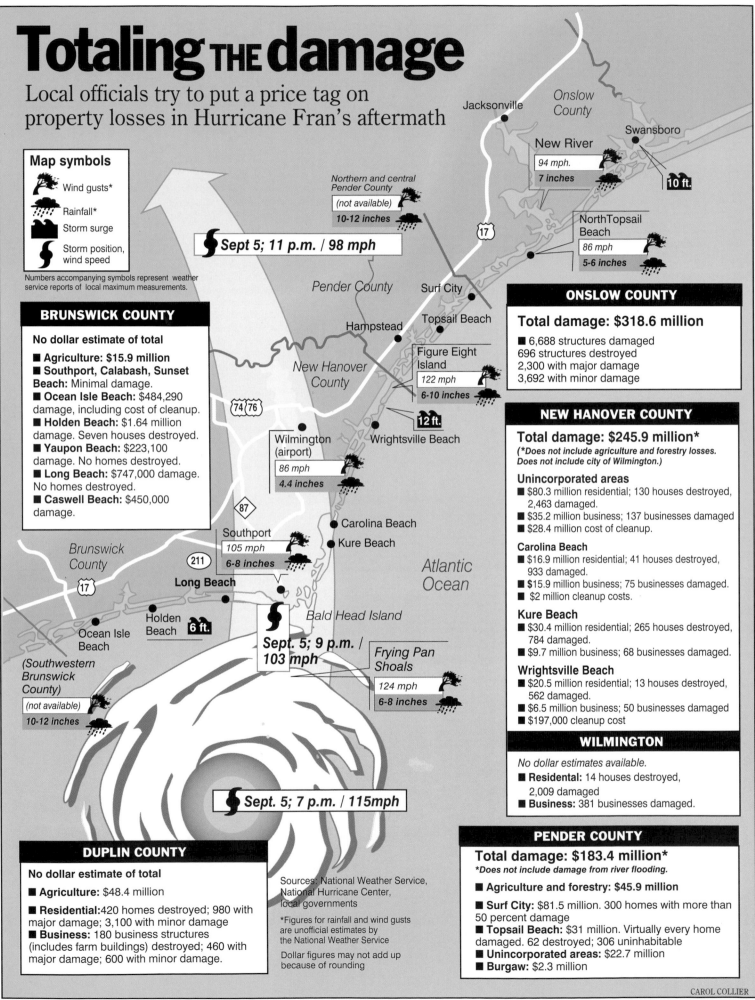

Map symbols

- Wind gusts*
- Rainfall*
- Storm surge
- Storm position, wind speed

Numbers accompanying symbols represent weather service reports of local maximum measurements.

Northern and central Pender County
(not available)
10-12 inches

Sept 5; 11 p.m. / 98 mph

Pender County

Surf City

Topsail Beach

Hampstead

New Hanover County

Figure Eight Island
122 mph
6-10 inches
12 ft.

Wrightsville Beach

Wilmington (airport)
86 mph
4.4 inches

Carolina Beach

Kure Beach

Southport
105 mph
6-8 inches

Long Beach

Atlantic Ocean

Bald Head Island

Sept. 5; 9 p.m. / 103 mph

Frying Pan Shoals
124 mph
6-8 inches

Onslow County

Jacksonville

Swansboro

New River
94 mph.
7 inches

10 ft.

NorthTopsail Beach
86 mph
5-6 inches

17

BRUNSWICK COUNTY

No dollar estimate of total

- **Agriculture: $15.9 million**
- **Southport, Calabash, Sunset Beach:** Minimal damage.
- **Ocean Isle Beach:** $484,290 damage, including cost of cleanup.
- **Holden Beach:** $1.64 million damage. Seven houses destroyed.
- **Yaupon Beach:** $223,100 damage. No homes destroyed.
- **Long Beach:** $747,000 damage. No homes destroyed.
- **Caswell Beach:** $450,000 damage.

Brunswick County

17

Holden Beach   6 ft.

Ocean Isle Beach

(Southwestern Brunswick County)
(not available)
10-12 inches

Sept. 5; 7 p.m. / 115mph

DUPLIN COUNTY

No dollar estimate of total

- **Agriculture: $48.4 million**

- **Residential:** 420 homes destroyed; 980 with major damage; 3,100 with minor damage
- **Business:** 180 business structures (includes farm buildings) destroyed; 460 with major damage; 600 with minor damage.

Sources: National Weather Service, National Hurricane Center, local governments

*Figures for rainfall and wind gusts are unofficial estimates by the National Weather Service

Dollar figures may not add up because of rounding

ONSLOW COUNTY

Total damage: $318.6 million

- 6,688 structures damaged
  696 structures destroyed
  2,300 with major damage
  3,692 with minor damage

NEW HANOVER COUNTY

Total damage: $245.9 million*
*(*Does not include agriculture and forestry losses. Does not include city of Wilmington.)*

Unincorporated areas
- $80.3 million residential; 130 houses destroyed, 2,463 damaged.
- $35.2 million business; 137 businesses damaged
- $28.4 million cost of cleanup.

Carolina Beach
- $16.9 million residential; 41 houses destroyed, 933 damaged.
- $15.9 million business; 75 businesses damaged.
- $2 million cleanup costs.

Kure Beach
- $30.4 million residential; 265 houses destroyed, 784 damaged.
- $9.7 million business; 68 businesses damaged.

Wrightsville Beach
- $20.5 million residential; 13 houses destroyed, 562 damaged.
- $6.5 million business; 50 businesses damaged
- $197,000 cleanup cost

WILMINGTON

No dollar estimates available.

- **Residental:** 14 houses destroyed, 2,009 damaged
- **Business:** 381 businesses damaged.

PENDER COUNTY

Total damage: $183.4 million*
Does not include damage from river flooding.

- **Agriculture and forestry: $45.9 million**

- **Surf City:** $81.5 million. 300 homes with more than 50 percent damage
- **Topsail Beach:** $31 million. Virtually every home damaged. 62 destroyed; 306 uninhabitable
- **Unincorporated areas:** $22.7 million
- **Burgaw:** $2.3 million

CAROL COLLIER

TODD SUMLIN

Day after day of heavy rainstorms caused widespread flooding near the Northeast Cape Fear River. Brothers Daniel (left) and Oral Ramsey seemed overwhelmed at Daniel's riverfront home between Rocky Point and Burgaw.

ALONG CAME A MANATEE

Four pairs of eyes were pressed against a window watching Hurricane Fran take out its fury on Carolina Beach.

"I'm looking at the sound right now, and it looks like the ocean," said Granger Soward from his Canal Drive home.

Mr. Soward and four friends and neighbors watched as water rolled into his yard and covered his mailbox. A black Pontiac was swept up by the current and pushed into a house.

About 9:30 p.m., Fran was quiet as the eye of the storm passed, giving them a chance to go outside to survey the damage. From the swirling floodwaters at the base of his house, he saw an amazing sight.

"As God is my witness, we have a manatee right here at the back door," Mr. Soward said. He and his friends watched the manatee for about an hour before it turned and headed for deeper water.

"I knew nobody would believe us," he said. "And we're sitting here without a camera."

humbled by Fran's obvious power.

Before floodwaters receded, people began wondering just how Hurricane Fran ranked in state history, particularly whether it compared to Hurricane Hazel, long the benchmark of any hurricane in this part of the country.

Fran was responsible for 25 deaths, while Hazel killed 95. Fran caused far more property damage. In North Carolina alone, Hazel caused $136 million in damage, though those figures are in 1954 dollars.

But from a meteorological point of view, Fran was no Hazel. The great storm of 1954 is still the only Category 4 storm to hit North Carolina, with 150-mph winds and an 18-foot storm surge that came in on a full moon high tide, approaching homes' second floors. In Long Beach, Hazel practically erased the town, destroying 325 of 357 buildings.

Fran can't even claim that kind of damage at Topsail Island, though newer buildings can stand heavier winds.

Hurricane activity seems to be picking up, and some forecasters believe the area is due for another cycle of heavy storms, much like 1954-55, when four hit the North Carolina coast.

But chances are that no one alive for the summer of 1996 will live to see a Hazel, or maybe even another Fran.

Chances are even better that no one wants to.

'I'D LIKE TO SIT THROUGH ONE. I JUST WANT TO SEE NATURE.'

Gary Clark of Charlotte, explaining why he intended to ride out Hurricane Fran
at his father's home in Holden Beach despite an evacuation order

KEN BLEVINS

Workers at Carolina Yacht Club in Wrightsville Beach secure boats as Fran heads for shore.

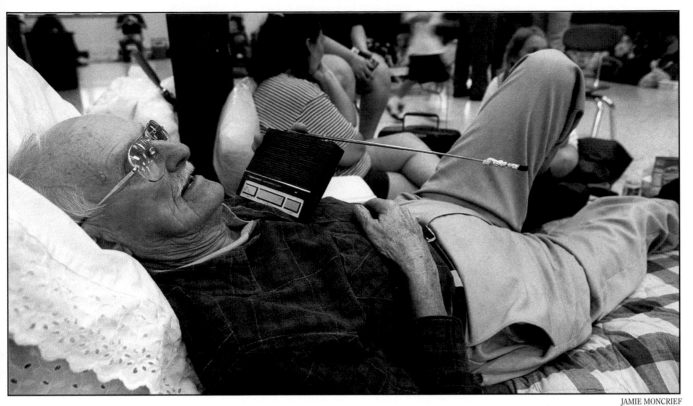

Bige Eversole, 76, of Long Beach listens to weather reports on Hurricane Fran by radio at an evacuation shelter at South Brunswick High School.

Heavy rains in advance of Hurricane Fran didn't stop a soggy football game for these UNC-Wilmington students just hours before the storm made landfall.

RISKY BUSINESS

As Fran battered Carolina Beach, Dorina Risk, 70, chose to stay in her two-story cottage with her 82-year-old husband, her son and her granddaughter.

"My husband has Parkinson's," she explained. "You take him to the shelter and people stare and gawk."

With Mr. Risk too weak to go upstairs, the family tried to fight off the water surge on the first floor by piling furniture in front of the door. Her son tried to hold the door.

"When that gush of water came in, it knocked him down," Mrs. Risk said.

After the storm, she dug family photos out of a layer of mud that covered her floor.

"Material things," she said. "You realize when this happens, a human life is worth much more."

A Carolina Beach house becomes an island as water laps around its bottom floor.
Waves carried away air conditioners, washing machines and vinyl siding from homes in the area.

MATTRESS IN THE MARSH

Georgia Greene's experience with Hurricane Fran must have been something like her life – lonely.

The 75-year-old Surf City woman was bedridden and depended on round-the-clock nurses. She lost her husband in 1993, had no children and had lost touch with most other relatives.

The day after Fran struck, rescue workers found Mrs. Greene on a mattress in the marsh across the street from her demolished mobile home. Family members didn't know why the nurses left her.

But some say Mrs. Greene didn't want to leave her home. When Hurricane Bertha hit in July, she stuck it out.

Rescue workers believe Mrs. Greene was out most of the night in the churning waters pushed up by Fran. She was taken to Columbia Cape Fear Hospital in Wilmington, where she died the next day.

Tim Powell, who lived on Atkinson Point Road across the Intracoastal Waterway from Mrs. Greene, reported hearing a voice on the night of Sept. 5 at the height of Hurricane Fran.

Could it have been Mrs. Greene?

Mr. Powell heard the voice only once. He said he never dreamed it might be a stranded person.

KEN BLEVINS

Trailer homes were tossed about like Matchbox cars at Topsail Island.

Like a child playing with toys in a bathtub, Hurricane Fran tossed recreational boats about at area marinas. Total damage to boats was estimated at $40 to $50 million. This was the scene at Masonboro Boat Yard.

KEN BLEVINS

Both Confederate and Union troops used the steeple at First Baptist Church as a lookout, depending on which side was occupying the city during the Civil War. Hurricane Fran brought the 197-foot spire to the ground.

FRIENDS OF FRAN

As he sat outside a Red Cross shelter at Dixon Middle School in Onslow County, Hank Henderson was feeling pretty lucky.

"Most of the people here are a whole lot worse off than me," said Mr. Henderson, 58, a maintenance worker at North Topsail Beach. "I've still got a place to live and a job, hopefully."

His roommate at the shelter, 78-year-old John Kurowski, lost almost everything to Hurricane Fran. His bottom-floor apartment in North Topsail Beach was destroyed.

The two men passed their days at the shelter sitting outside or reading a box of *National Geographic* magazines a school custodian gave them.

"I don't like to talk much," Mr. Henderson said, "but he does. So we have had some pretty interesting talks about the articles in those magazines."

The two men had never met before the storm.

"I guess some good has come of this hurricane," Mr. Henderson said.

National Guardsmen were sent to patrol Kure Beach, as well as other areas hard hit by Hurricane Fran.

Although access to beaches was limited, looters used boats to get to some damaged areas.

What was once a third-floor kitchen was the only room left intact when Steve Currie returned to his Kure Beach home. The house was crushed by Fran into a pile of lumber. Sifting through the debris, he salvaged family photos and coloring books. 'If I had the money, I'd move into a hotel room and never own anything again,' he mused.

'IT'S A DISASTER. THERE'S A HOUSE IN THE MIDDLE OF THE ROAD.'

Surf City Police Officer Ron Shanahan, surveying damage a day after Fran hit

JAMIE MONCRIEF

Surf City residents found massive devastation when they returned to their homes.
TODD SUMLIN

STORMY BEGINNINGS

Long before Hurricane Fran was even a tropical depression, Hope Hall had chosen what turned out to be the perfect name for her baby boy.

Davin Storm Alexander Hall, a healthy 10-pounder, was born at 6:54 p.m. Sept. 5 as the hurricane raged outside Columbia Brunswick Hospital at Supply.

The baby will be called Storm.

"I couldn't have picked out a better name, I think," the 21-year-old mother said.

Hours after Storm was born, another baby arrived in dramatic fashion in Bladen County. Firefighters used chain saws to clear a path for rescue workers to get to the mother's home. Adding to the urgency was the fact that it was a breech birth.

The emergency call came in just after midnight. Ambulances had stopped running because of the dangerous storm conditions.

Calls to hospitals and military bases for a medical helicopter were futile because most choppers had been moved to safety out of state.

So crews from four area rescue squads started toward the mother's home from different directions. Firefighters drove in front of the ambulances to clear fallen trees in the way. It took 53 minutes for rescuers from Kelly to travel 10 miles. A Bladen County deputy escorted an ambulance to the county hospital, where the baby was delivered.

Mother and child were reported fine.

Water from nearby Hewlett's Creek flooded Daryl Bowers' home in the Shamrock Village neighborhood. Heavy rains in the days after Fran hit added to the misery of residents who lost everything.

'THREE-HUNDRED-SIXTY-FOUR DAYS A YEAR, IT'S BEAUTIFUL OUT HERE.'

Charlie Lechel, who fled his mobile home in the Myrtle Grove area to stay in a motel. He returned to find his home destroyed.

John Pike and Barbie Thompson survey their water-soaked apartment at Wrightsville Beach. Water rose to a level above the doorknob. They lost most of their possessions, including a record collection.

TYLER HICKS

Sections of Lake Park Boulevard in Carolina Beach collapsed. Parts of the street were under 6 feet of water by 9 p.m. Sept. 5.

TYLER HICKS

Fran dumped a 3-foot layer of sand over the Boardwalk in Carolina Beach. A town police officer patrols the area a day after the storm.

COFFEE AND ANGELS

Hot coffee and working gas pumps.

That's what the Pantry at Wellington Avenue and South 17th Street offered a day after Hurricane Fran.

Perhaps because it is on the "hospital grid," the convenience store was one of a few in Wilmington that had electricity restored so quickly.

An employee assigned to "brew detail" efficiently filled filters and poured for a steady line of 20 coffee customers who had lost electricity at home.

Across the street at Greenlawn Memorial Park, Beulah Giddens stood near her husband's grave replacing red silk carnations in a bronze vase toppled by the storm.

"We went through Hazel together," she said. "I like to think that John's my guardian angel. I don't know if I really believe that, but it's a nice something to hold onto."

The main road on exclusive Figure Eight Island was plowed after Fran buried it under sand. Many oceanfront houses had major damage. Ground-floor levels were washed out by the storm surge, and protective dunes were flattened.

State legislators got a look at damage on Topsail Island during a helicopter tour Sept. 10, and this is what they saw. 'We need to get out with the least amount of cost possible and don't come back,' said Sen. Marc Basnight, D-Dare. 'You just can't live in certain parts of the coast. They're not made for homes.'

'I KNOW THERE WERE HOUSES IN THOSE SPOTS BEFORE I CROSSED THE BRIDGE. THERE WERE JUST SEPTIC TANKS THERE TODAY.'

Holden Beach Town Manager Sean Anderson, who allowed that damage in his area could have been much worse

KEN BLEVINS

At low tide, sailboats are strewn at the Bradley Creek bridge on Oleander Drive after Hurricane Bertha damaged Bradley Creek Marina, ripping up part of a dock.

> **'THEY'RE EITHER GOING TO LEARN TO BARK, OR SHE'LL LEARN TO CLIMB TREES.'**
> Cathy Nunalee

TODD SUMLIN

Chloe and her new charges.

ORPHANS OF THE STORM

Cathy Nunalee didn't have the slightest idea how to care for a nest of baby squirrels that fell in a neighbor's yard during Hurricane Fran.

She needn't have worried. Her 5-year-old Yorkshire terrier, Chloe, adopted the blind infants.

Ms. Nunalee discovered the squirrels when she went to a neighbor's house for coffee. The storm had knocked down a tree in the neighbor's yard, throwing the squirrels from their nest.

Wildlife rehabilitators were unable to help, but did advise her on what to feed the babies. Ms. Nunalee heated water bottles on a grill to warm an eyedropper that she would use for feeding.

Then Chloe hopped into a suitcase where the squirrels were lying. The pooch, twice a mother, hadn't had a litter in two years. But she seemed to be nursing the squirrels.

"I thought, what stupid little squirrels," a surprised Ms. Nunalee said.

A quick inspection confirmed that Chloe was producing milk and the squirrels were getting fed.

Ms. Nunalee planned to take the squirrels to a wildlife rehabilitator when they were ready to be weaned.

Lila Covil locked the doors and sealed the windows of her 150-year-old home in Burgaw on Sept. 4, then headed for her son's home in Durham to escape Hurricane Fran. When the 82-year-old returned three days later, she started packing again. The roof was ripped off, and a huge oak had crashed onto the house. Friends and family helped salvage belongings.

Beachgoers search for shells in front of a home that collapsed at Holden Beach.

Carolina Beach Police Chief Mike Mayer salvages what he can in his storm-wrecked office. The Police Department was forced to move to the town recreation center after its Canal Drive headquarters was smashed. A new police-fire station will have to be built.

'THE WORST THING IS HAVING KIDS WITH NO WATER. YOU CAN'T WASH YOUR HANDS, FLUSH THE TOILET. YOU JUST FEEL DIRTY.'

Sharon Helton, who had almost finished clearing debris from Hurricane Bertha at her Middle Sound area home when Fran knocked down more than 20 trees

Through rain, hail, sleet, maybe – but not through 3 feet of sand. Mailboxes are nearly covered after Fran dumped sand into the streets of Carolina Beach.

Matt Woods (left) and Jason Kane survey damage at Scotts Hill Marina on Sept. 6.
Before Fran, the marina was scheduled to be used as a location for the movie
'Buried Alive II.' Producers agreed to foot half the bill for a new
floating dock to help get the marina in shape for filming.

A huge oak tree was toppled on Nash Street in Southport.

A farmhouse off N.C. 53 in Pender County is surrounded by floodwaters a week after Hurricane Fran.

AND THEN CAME THE FLOODS

JAMIE MONCRIEF

Michelle Massey wades out of River Bend subdivision near the Northeast Cape Fear River, which flooded the area with 8 feet of water in the days after Fran.

TYLER HICKS

Jennifer Coombs' well was under water, so her family wasn't drinking from it two weeks after Hurricane Fran. Flooding that followed the storm created misery for families near the Northeast Cape Fear River.

Nathan Booth (left) rides a bike through 4 feet of water Sept. 11 in the NorthChase subdivision. Heavy rains in the week after Fran caused flooding throughout the region, adding misery to cleanup chores.

'GROUND'S SO WET, IT'S GOT NOWHERE TO GO. I'M THINKING OF GOING TO GET ME AN ARK.'

Robert Andrews , whose Sharon Drive home was drenched again when heavy rains soaked the area three days after Fran passed through

Annie Bannerman's porch was the driest around in the Burgaw Creek community Sept. 6, so neighbors gathered there to be ferried to dry land on N.C. 53. Water was a foot deep inside Ms. Bannerman's home. 'It's something,' said her 78-year-old mother, Dora Bryant.

Nancy Tatum ties her canoe to a mailbox post just off Cape Fear Drive outside Burgaw. Her home was overcome by flooding, and she was on the way to a store for supplies.

Floating trees and branches created a logjam on the Brunswick River near the U.S. 74-76 bridge at Leland. A state Department of Transportation barge with crane was sent to clear the way.

HIGH HOPES DROWNED

Busted.

That's what a lot of coastal marijuana farmers were in the wake of hurricanes Fran and Bertha.

Fran drowned or toppled much of a bumper crop of the drug hidden in area marshes and along rivers. And because of a long, fruitful growing season preceding the hurricanes, stalks were taller than usual and thus easier for helicopter-borne drug agents to spot.

In its first post-Fran helicopter bust about two weeks after the storm, Brunswick County sheriff's deputies pulled up a pickup load of 68 stalks, some more than twice as tall as the deputies.

Hurricane Fran hit at peak harvest time for marijuana, law enforcement officers said. Marijuana growers like to hide their crops along rivers, streams and marshes — areas particularly susceptible to storm flooding.

'I'VE SEEN WHEN YOU HAD TO BOAT IN AND OUT IN 1924. I THINK IT'S ABOUT AT A STAND.'

Dewey Long, 83, of Crusoe Island, where water stood 3 feet deep Sept. 11 on the road 100 yards from his house

Tommy Spivey describes the depth of water in his Crusoe Island home. Like many island residents, known as an independent lot, Mr. Spivey did not plan to evacuate.

How high was the water? Street signs in the River Bend subdivision in Pender County were nearly submerged.

On Sept. 12, rain was still falling near Riegelwood at an already overwhelmed Lock and Dam No. 1, which is barely visible here as floodwaters charge over the site.

TOWING THE LINE

For drivers who got stuck in the rising post-Fran floodwaters along N.C. 53, Green's Wrecker Service of Maple Hill was a lifesaver.

Business was booming, rescuing people and dragging their cars out of troubled water.

Travis Green said he just couldn't understand why people would drive into the cola-colored water, which was waist-deep in areas between Maple Hill and Interstate 40.

"I ain't never seen it like this," Mr. Green said.

Angela Chisholm thought her Ford Probe would make it. She was wrong.

Mr. Green pulled up as she sat atop her car with a cellular telephone. "I was calling my husband," she said. "I was driving along and it just died. Then all this water started coming up, and I got scared. Climbing on top of my car seemed like a good plan."

Green's Wrecker pulled in 28 vehicles over two days, at $150 a pop.

"It's extra if there's a snakebite involved," owner Leslie Green said with a laugh.

Bradley Ramsey and his family and neighbors were forced to seek higher ground after their White Oak Road homes in Pender County were flooded by water from the Northeast Cape Fear River.

TODD SUMLIN

Parts of N.C. 50 in Topsail Beach were eaten away by the force of Hurricane Fran.

Workers began the task of putting the Kure Beach Pier back together a week after Hurricane Fran destroyed what was left by Hurricane Bertha.

KEN BLEVINS

'IF YOU WANT THE BENEFITS OF LIVING AT THE BEACH, YOU HAVE TO TAKE THE GOOD WITH THE NEGATIVE.'

Marlow Bostic, a developer at North Topsail Beach who has often been criticized as having little regard for coastal development rules

BE REBUILT?

In the aftermath of Hurricanes Bertha and Fran, local officials and state policymakers faced tough questions on development along the battered, fragile coastline.

On many beaches, Fran washed over sea oats and dunes, the first line of vegetation from which houses are typically set back 60 feet.

The N.C. Coastal Resources Commission decided to allow state officials to use a patchwork of aerial photography and ground observations to establish building setbacks.

Regulators called it a compromise between two extremes: using a pre-Bertha line or forbidding immediate rebuilding.

Still, officials faced the sensitive task of telling a large percentage of some 1,000 beachfront homeowners that they will not be allowed to rebuild.

On another issue, the commission seemed unwilling to compromise. Owners at Shell Island Resort in Wrightsville Beach wanted to place sandbags around the $22 million condo hotel in a bid to keep it from falling into the ocean because of erosion. On Sept. 28, 1996, the commission rejected that request, adhering to a state policy that bans seawalls.

The ruling was subject to appeal.

'IF I LIVE TO SEE ANOTHER ONE, I'M HEADING FOR THE HILLS.'

Doris Culverhouse, 78, who with her husband, Bill, rode out Bertha at their Carolina Beach home

TYLER HICKS

Chad Rhodes struggles up a mountain of sand to reach a walkway that used to lead to the beach at Surf City. Erosion from Hurricane Fran wiped out dunes.

A surfer shares the beach with a construction vehicle in the aftermath of Hurricane Bertha.

'I THINK IT'S GOD'S WAY OF SHOWING US WHO'S BOSS.'

Mable Earley, whose oceanfront cottage at North Topsail Beach was destroyed

A Surf City house teeters on the edge of a 4-foot cliff on the beach, where dunes were eroded by Hurricane Fran.

Mason Inlet brushes ever closer to Shell Island Resort at Wrightsville Beach. A 6-foot dune that separated the sidewalk from the inlet was washed away, leaving little protection for the $22 million hotel.

PLAYING THROUGH

From Glenn Sasser's Surf City home, Hurricane Fran plucked a television set, VCR, an answering machine, three beds and lots of clothes.

But the storm didn't get his golf clubs.

"When I was walking out the door, I don't know why, but I said, 'I better get my golf clubs,'" the New Hanover High School football coach said.

"The reason I didn't get my TV is because it was raining," he said. "But I said, 'Look, clubs can get wet. They've been wet before.' So I threw them in the back of my truck."

The day after the storm, Mr. Sasser chartered a plane to fly over Surf City. His home was destroyed.

"It's unreal," he said. "If you could see where my place was, you would not think you were in America. You would think you were in Beirut."

A helicopter lifts a fallen tree in the Porters Neck area a week after Hurricane Fran knocked over more than 500 trees in the area. The company that owns the chopper, Atlas Storm Troopers, specializes in debris cleanup after natural disasters. Atlas had about four weeks' worth of work lined up at area golf courses and other sites.

TYLER HICKS

Ice was a hot commodity for people without electricity to run refrigerators and freezers.
The wait was more than two hours Sept. 7 at Rose Ice and Coal on Market Street.

PICKING UP THE PIECES

'THIS IS THE GENERATOR LINE.'

Larry Powell
of Carolina Beach,
lined up with
200 others at Lowe's
home store a day
after Hurricane
Fran's strike

Volunteers poured into the area in the aftermath of both hurricanes.
Audrey Nance of Franklinville, near Asheboro, serves a meal
for Mack Whitmore at a Red Cross station at Topsail High
School, where more than 21,000 were fed the Sunday
after Bertha swept through.

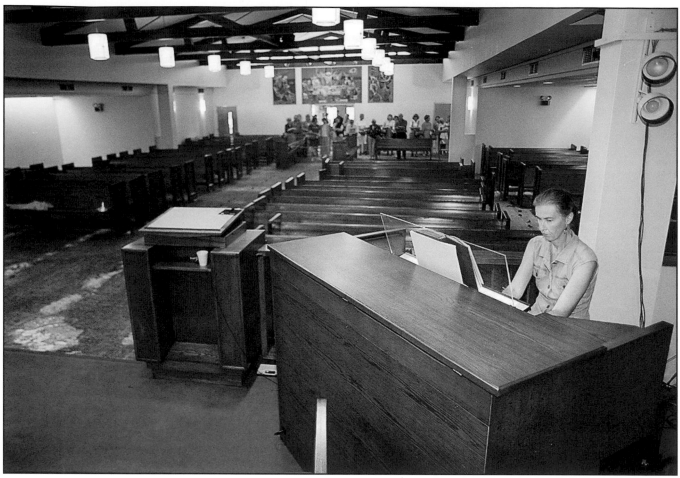

KEN BLEVINS

'All Hail the Power of Jesus' Name' swelled from the organ as Mary Nelson Smith played for services at Little Chapel on the Boardwalk in Wrightsville Beach. Church members gathered in the parking lot for Sept. 16 services. Afterward, they crowded into the back of the flood-damaged sanctuary to hear the new organ, which was undamaged.

'IN A SITUATION LIKE THIS, I'D RATHER SHOOT FIRST AND ASK QUESTIONS LATER.'

Charlie Rivenbark, member of the Wilmington City Council, which passed an anti-price gouging ordinance two days after Fran. The city attorney had questioned whether the action was legal

JAMIE MONCRIEF

Restaurants and bars had to shorten nighttime hours when the city imposed a 10 p.m.-6 a.m. curfew for four days after Hurricane Fran. A similar order had followed Bertha. City officials said that without electricity, it would be hard for police to maintain security. Some business owners criticized the curfews, with one bar owner saying he lost $30,000 in sales after Fran.

THE'N. PHAM

Dave Wicker of West Virginia rests after a long day of trucking storm debris at a camp for cleanup workers on a vacant Market Street lot. Dozens of workers who came for post-hurricane jobs saved money by camping out rather than stay in motels. 'What makes it hard is bathing,' Mr. Wicker said.

JAMIE MONCRIEF

Tree service workers from Asplundh's Florida group were among crews from across the country that came to help in the storm cleanup and restoring power.

POWER TO THE FISHES

Marine life at the N.C. Aquarium at Fort Fisher was saved, thanks in part to the wife of a Carolina Power & Light Co. employee.

In the days following Hurricane Fran, the aquarium used diesel-powered generators to keep water circulating in its fish tanks. After a couple of days, fuel was running low. Without power, the aquarium staff faced the difficult task of releasing a marine life collection that took years to build.

But after reading of the aquarium's plight in the Sept. 8 Morning Star, the CP&L worker's wife told her husband that if he was going to do anything that day, it would be to restore power to the aquarium.

By 11 a.m., electricity was back on.

Aquarium curator Paul Barrington said he received dozens of calls from people willing to donate fuel and generators to keep the fish tanks running.

"I'm humbled," he said. "Disasters bring out the best in people."

OUR STORMY PAST

While predictions of hurricanes have grown more sophisticated, it is still impossible to say exactly when and where one will hit.

Until Bertha struck in July 1996, the worst hurricane to hit Southeastern North Carolina in recent years had been Diana in September 1984. It left about $79 million in damage, concentrated in southern New Hanover County and the beach areas of Brunswick County.

Long the benchmark for hurricanes in the region, Hurricane Hazel – now rivaled in destructive force by Fran – slammed into Oak Island in October 1954 with 150-mph wind and a 17-foot storm surge.

Hazel destroyed virtually every building on Long Beach. It then continued through the mid-Atlantic states, killing 95 people and causing millions of dollars in damage.

Stanley Goodman wades through water-filled streets at Carolina Beach on Sept. 13, 1984, during Hurricane Diana.

Hurricane Hazel slammed the Carolina coast in 1954. This is the north end of Carolina Beach.

TYLER HICKS

Rex Bennett packs dirt into a doorway as he prepares to ride out Hurricane Fran at Carolina Beach. The building survived Hurricane Hazel in 1954.

The Savage Season is based on coverage of Hurricanes Bertha and Fran in the Wilmington Morning Star.

CHARLES M. ANDERSON
 EXECUTIVE EDITOR
JOHN H. MEYER
 MANAGING EDITOR

DAVE ENNIS
 CITY EDITOR
JANET ROBERTS, GIL AEGERTER
 ASSISTANT CITY EDITORS
SCOTT WHISNANT
 REGIONAL EDITOR
JOSIAH CANTWELL
 BUSINESS EDITOR
PAM SANDER
 LIFESTYLE EDITOR
MIKE BOAZ
 SPORTS EDITOR
THE' N. PHAM
 CHIEF PHOTOGRAPHER

DONNA PIPES
 NEWS EDITOR
SCOTT NUNN
 ASSISTANT NEWS EDITOR
BOBBY PARKER
 SPECIAL PROJECTS EDITOR

KIRSTEN B. MITCHELL
 RALEIGH BUREAU CHIEF

STAFF WRITERS:
 DANA ALLWEIN, KRISTINA BARTLETT,
 MAILE CARPENTER, CHUCK CARREE,
 VICTORIA CHERRIE, CLIFTON DANIEL,
 CHRIS DAVIS, BETTIE FENNELL,
 RODNEY FOUSHEE, PHILIP HERVEY,
 DEIRDRE MCGRUDER,
 MARTY MINCHIN, CELIA RIVENBARK,
 HOLLY ROBERSON, LEE ROBERTS,
 PAUL R. SCHMIDT, JEFF SELINGO,
 TRICIA VANCE, CLAUDINE R. WILLIAMS

COPY EDITORS:
 SUSAN BREWTON, WILL JONES,
 STEVE MCDANIEL, LEE NANCE,
 JAY NIVER, TRACY ORMSBEE,
 DOUG ROBERSON, MERTON VANCE

PHOTOGRAPHERS:
 KEN BLEVINS, TYLER HICKS,
 JAMIE MONCRIEF, TODD SUMLIN

NEWS ARTIST
 CAROL COLLIER

LIBRARY STAFF:
 MARY MACCALLUM, KIM HORD

TV REPORTER
 CHERYL WHITAKER

NEWS CLERKS:
 MARY BURCH, FRANCESCA EVANS,
 JEANNIE HENDERSON

NEWS CORRESPONDENTS:
 MISTI C. LEE, ANNE MINARD,
 JAY MOYE, JEFFERSON WEAVER

A man rides a bicycle through the flooded streets of Carolina Beach as Hurricane Fran bears down.

WE TOOK A LICKING, BUT KEEP ON TICKING

It's no comfort to know it could have been worse. It was plenty bad enough.

The area has been vandalized on a huge scale. Residential neighborhoods, just relieved of their Bertha debris, are again littered with fallen trees, power lines and smashed transformers. The First Baptist Church lost its steeple.

Then there are the beaches. They always get by far the worst of these blows, of course. Up and down the strands, piers are gone and boats are scattered.

The good news, if you can call it that, is that houses weren't smashed one after another, as they were in 1954. But the water and mud have done their destructive work.

It is one unholy mess.

No sooner had the sun risen the day after the storm than Wilmingtonians were beavering away in their yards, cleaning up what they could. Chain saws were snarling and generators were droning. Public employees were on the job.

Fran knocked us down, but not for long. Now we're in for another long siege of cutting up the wreckage and hauling it away.

The roofing and tree service outfits will be up to their bill caps in work. The insurance adjusters will be frowning and mopping their brows.

And will the electricity be on? Probably not for a good while for a good many of us.

It's at times like these that the city of Wilmington's motto seems to speak to us with particular relevance: Persevere.

From an editorial in the Wilmington Morning Star, Sept. 7, 1996